AWAKENING
TO
REMEMBERING

A Journey of Consciousness

LISA "TRANSCENDENCE" BROWN

Translating the Energies of "They" as "WE"

DEDICATION

To all who are awakening to remembering that which has been forgotten. May this assist you further on your journey into your own soul and beyond.

CONTENTS

ACKNOWLEDGMENTS

I acknowledge that I am but a vessel for consciousness and in this space WE all exist as one. It is in this space that I share with you.

REMEMBERING

As all are here to remember, this is to assist in that journey of the **Forgotten World**. You are embraced in every moment with the absolute highest love that is offered and can be achieved; the space of oneness. It is here that all seek and will come to understand.

LIGHT IS SIMPLE

There is much to cover here, but by much we mean simplify. This book need not be massive, as that would be the writings of the human mind.

SLEEP & WAKING STATE

In your reality, you close your eyes to sleep and open your eyes to wake. This is because your logical mind is present when your eyes are open. When you learn to close your eyes, you will see. You see much in your sleep state, but your mind does not allow you to see. As your realities merge, your states will become interchangeable. Sleep and wake state, for awhile, will be confusing. But it is this transition that is imperative to your ability to remember. It is when your mind shuts down that you are able to connect to that which will become your natural state.

There will be many periods when all you can do is sleep. Honor this. Your DNA is restructuring, cellular memory repatterning, Light Codes are activating, energies assimilating and your physical is healing. Your consciousness will integrate the more you allow yourself to sleep.

WORDS

Words are only necessary in human form. They are necessary to write this book so that the human spirit can read it and understand from a thinking and logical perspective. We ask that you absorb this book into your being and that you feel it instead of think. As you absorb it, your energy will process it as a frequency received rather than a thought formed to understand it.

As one elevates in consciousness, words have no meaning. They are used only to describe that which the logical mind comprehends. For this sake, words will be used only to describe. They will hold the energy that you attribute to them according to your own reality.

Words of duality have been limited here, for they differ based on one's own level of understanding & consciousness. Since they only exist in separation, then they are addressed as so. One may see these in lower frequency perspectives as right/wrong, good/bad, dark/light, fear/love, etc.

Words are interchangeable much of the time and are used very loosely. You will need to choose words that assist you in your own understanding. We have chosen a few "common" ones for the sake of bridging the communication barriers that you have created among yourselves.

Human Self: Ego, Rational Mind, Thinking Mind, Logical Mind, Physical Mind, Lower Self, Individual. (Linear)

Energetic Being/Body/Self: Soul, Spirit, Higher Self, Light Being, Multi-Dimensional Self, Higher Consciousness, ONE. (Non-Linear)

We will use them interchangeably and leave it up to you to determine what feels right for you. Much of the time we will just speak of you as energy or an energetic being, as this is what you are.

WORDS OF LIGHT

There is no reason to speak except as descriptive to help one understand that which the logical mind needs to comprehend. Not speaking allows one to go within to listen to the words of their own soul in order to guide them on their own journey as they chose to experience it.

Words of Light are used to uplift, assist in healing and purely for the transmission of light. They do not speak of an individual, as they are of the consciousness of ONE. Your language will change to one of a frequency transmission as you continue to expand.

Silence is perfection, as communication of the heart requires no spoken words.

SEPARATION OF CONSCIOUSNESS

You exist as one consciousness already. As a human form, you take on duality by way of your logical & thinking mind. This logic separates your consciousness and as you work to transcend the limits of your own human mind, you "work" to find your way "home". Home is within you and is a state of being that you once knew. How soon you remember will be determined by your ability to embrace, allow, release and stretch your own limits according to thought.

You are not "going anywhere". You are already here.

SEPARATION FROM SOURCE

At the very highest level there is no separation. There is only ONENESS.

Imagine stepping out of ONENESS into separation. This is how we will describe separation. It occurs as the soul descends from a place of creation. We address all from a point of descension, as this is how one may view it. From the human's view, it is one of ascension. As all attempt to integrate, it is seen as one of expansion. This will change for each as they evolve as a Being of Light.

The further one separates, the lower the frequency one operates. So at any given time, one can choose to integrate more, bring in more light and allow for separation to fall away. The limits placed on this are of the human ego, which was created to act out your own duality that you chose before ever "leaving" here to exist as a separate energetic being.

You exist in consciousness. As more remember this, they will elevate in consciousness to embody their pure Divine Essence. The physical reality you see is manifested by that of your own logical mind. The more power you give to the physical, the more power it holds over your ability to exist as a Being of Light, keeping you further separated.

SEPARATION OF TIME

In human form, yours is a journey that has been separated by "time". Here you measure time by past, present, future, other lives, different dimensions, timelines and more.

There is no separation in time, just how you experience it. As you learn to become present in this moment at all times, all time exists here with you. You see this as a shift, because it is so foreign to you in the sleep (forgotten) state.

Time does not exist here. There is only one moment and each moment is but a different version than the one before.

The logical mind separates time into past, present, future. The more separated one's reality is, the more distance in "time" one perceives.

You exist as energy in a space where time does not exist. For even in this state, that one moment falls away and all just is.

SEPARATION OF REALITIES

For the purpose of the human experience there, you each have chosen your own reality to experience, grow through, heal and transcend. Again, this one is opposite than your physical perception. You think that all is separate, yet you intertwine your realities with each other, creating a dependency in this separation. It is not until you can separate your dependency and become responsible and present in your own reality, that you can exist in peace with all things as one.

SEPARATION OF SELVES

At the lowest frequency level, you have separated your "selves" out into different entities. There are so many that your logical mind cannot see, nor can it comprehend them all. There are selves that you have no idea exist. These are the core selves that surface during your journey. The further separated within, the further the self seems to be.

Your logical mind has created identities with jobs, others, relationships, memories, things. It cannot comprehend that all selves are one. You have placed the deepest fears in identities that you perceive as "far" away, like other dimensions, lifetimes or the spiritual world. You are not yet able to comprehend that all of those things are you.

6

For each separation, an emotion has been created. Separation results in suppression, depression and addiction, which result in every response imaginable. As you learn to release these identities of separation, you are able to recall those pieces of your own energy that feel "broken off", back to you for integration. You can replace dark with light, fear with love. You return to your true self for every untruth you release. For they are not anywhere else, yet a frequency in need of additional tuning.

This separation is a place of "dis-integration" there in the physical.

THOUGHTS OF SEPARATION

We do not wish to go into detail on every aspect of separation here. Humans have created way too many ways to be separate and this book would go on for what one perceives as forever. We will list some ways, and you can look inside and see if it applies to you. Choosing to embrace and release separation will allow for you to increase in frequency. Any identity that you choose to maintain will keep you separate that much longer.

"I" maintains separation. When one speaks from a WE standpoint and truly feels as one, all separation falls away. There is no competition, pride, measurement in WE. There is no ME in WE.

Now, many will fear this as a loss of self. It is through this understanding that one finds their true self. It is in maintaining I/Me that one is unable to see this. Through the dissolution of the individual, integration can continue to take place and ONENESS is truly achieved.

All individuals are special and perfect as a part of the whole.

SEEKING TRUTH

You have forgotten, and in your journey to remembering, you will take many paths to find your own truth. You always have access to truth within. You do not yet trust it, so you allow your logical mind to interfere with this. Here you create more experiences to learn from to arrive at the destination you seek.

You confuse yourself with thinking and lose focus. It is here that you will take what appears to be the indirect route to gather more experiences along the way. As you come to understand that this is your own distraction, you will learn to choose to listen to your own internal guidance. Even being distracted creates a beneficial experience in itself, for you scatter to seek more information to satisfy that of your logical mind. This further activates that within you that waits to wake. So as you can see, every moment assists you on your journey to remembering that which is dormant within.

You create your own barriers with your own thinking mind. You place obstacles in your own way to point you in the direction you seek. Where you do not trust and you follow the way of the human mind, you create additional experiences to show you that which you knew all along. There are actually no obstacles or barriers, only creations of new experiences in order to see.

You are being guided in every moment. Whether you create a perceived obstacle, walk through it, or completely understand that it does not exist, will be completely up to you. Every moment is an activation in itself.

MERGING REALITIES

Even these have separated into sleep and waking state, other dimensions, lifetimes and more. The more logical, the more these are separate. As these attempt to merge, the lines start to blur. One will feel confused and out of balance. Those beings in an awakening state will see sleep as a place to have strange dreams. These will graduate as one integrates to be lucid dreaming, astral traveling, then "experiences" and even to one interacting and working in their sleep. One will confuse waking & sleeping state and at times not know which is which. This too is part of the process of re-integration. One will see themselves in other dimensions, see other beings of other dimensions and see it as a profound experience, when in fact it is a remembering of that which is dormant within the separation of consciousness that attempt to re-emerge.

FREQUENCIES

You exist in frequency and the level of consciousness you are able to achieve and maintain will be dependent on your dominant frequency in any given moment. As you bring in more "light" and continue to elevate in frequency, you are able to maintain these higher frequencies and levels of consciousness for longer perceived periods of "time". When it is "time", all will merge and there will no longer be separation. Some call this connection to SOURCE, all that is, ONE. When the ego claims anything, it is done so as a part of your own separation.

Frequency is heard through sound and seen through light. You hear these frequencies in your head, but do not know what they are. In the beginning they will annoy you. This is because they act as a trigger to exacerbate sounds that will cause your lower frequencies to surface. Eventually, you learn to appreciate them as assistance and even use them to get confirmations and validation for certain things that you hear or speak through sound. They increase as your vibrational frequencies do and you start to understand more as you tap into that which you could not hear before.

They do not slow down. You increase your own vibrational spin to "speed up" to integrate with them as you become more light. In the beginning, many channel that which they receive. Automatic writing is one of the ways one does this. Over "time" one becomes one with this energy and there is no longer separation. Channeling is used only as a descriptive at this point. When one looks to something else for information, then they seek assistance as a separation from source. When one goes within, they no longer need to seek answers outside anymore.

The frequencies that you hear are your own frequencies as part of the whole, that work to attune you to a higher frequency as you expand into your own LightBody. They are the sound of Light as you perceive it in the physical. They increase as consciousness increases and logic falls away. The determined human can interfere with this by way of the need to hang on or control that which they experience or feel.

STREAMING ENERGIES

These energies can be heard and felt. We have already addressed how you hear them. You will also feel them in your physical body. How you feel them will depend on the "purpose" at that time, based upon your vibrational frequency.

These energies deliver Light Codes to your Energy Body. They activate that which is dormant within, to assist you in your remembering. This must be done over "time" as you perceive it, as your human mind could not take it otherwise.

When you are activated, it will feel like nervous energy to you. Where there is much to surface for clearing, then one may think they are having a panic attack. This is basically true, yet not. As the codes are activating your fears to surface. Where there are many, they will cause you to panic. Awareness of this allows you to breathe through it or take other measures not to suppress it.

There is much work being done to your physical body. You are being activated and tuned, which is seen as purging or clearing there. Your additional strands of DNA are also being activated, which allows for expansion into a new (remembered) space of consciousness for each strand as it activates.

These energies will cause the body to heat up for burning off and raising of one's vibrational frequencies. You are asked to sleep to allow for these codes to activate and integrate into your being, as your logical mind interferes and you must shut down to assimilate at a perceived faster rate.

As you bring in more light, you will come to appreciate these energies. They are transmitted from the Solar Sun as Photon Rays and other places you have yet to comprehend.

PHYSICAL MANIFESTATION

The physical world is your manifestation of your own frequencies. Your physical reality is a materialization of dense matter manifesting at a slower rate, therefore material things (including the human body) seem to appear at a much slower time frame than your linear mind can comprehend. The less linear, the "faster" manifestation appears to occur. So, where one is able to achieve a non-linear state majority of the time, the "faster" one perceives manifestation to be. This is dictated by your own vibrational frequency dictating the separation in time as you see it.

Where there is no separation in time, there also is no separation in creation and manifestation. It is only when you separate that you step back into waiting for anything.

SPACE OF CONSCIOUSNESS

The human sees in separation by way of levels, while the energetic being sees in a much more expansive view by way of perceptions and understandings, which expands with every "level" of consciousness that one observes from. One is "flat" and the other expands. This is exactly how duality works between these realities or worlds.

What or how you understand will be determined by the SPACE of consciousness you exist in. There are a multitude of answers to every question. Your ability to expand will determine how much you are able to see.

THE HOLOGRAM

We will speak of the hologram for a moment. With this view, you will also see that which others cannot see. You will see what is and is not real. Others may see you as emotionless, when in fact you understand beyond that which they can remember.

MEMORY STORAGE

The physical self created a memory by way of a perceived experience. In the physical, one thinks this is their reality, their memory, their individual experience. When in fact, the thought exists in a collective human consciousness that many "tap into" in order to experience their individual experience. This is why so many have the "same" experience, but with a variation of details according to that individual's created experience.

As one expands their consciousness to integrate at higher frequencies, how emotions are experienced and memories are accessed changes.

As one clears emotional attachments and thought energies, memories are released from the human's field and are accessible in the group consciousness. One can access these memories to assist another. They no longer hold an emotional charge and there is no reason to maintain them in one's individual energy field. As long as one holds onto separation, one will hold onto the memory as a part of their own individual identity.

As beings bring in more light, all that existed in the physical realms of lower vibration is able to leave one's energy field for "storage" in a memory field that all access from a higher state of consciousness. This is why many feel like they cannot remember. This is the case on a physical level, as memories are no longer stored in one's energy in the physical. They actually never were. They appeared to be present as they housed an emotion that needed to surface for the purpose of healing & releasing duality. They have been maintained by an energetic cord of attachment. When this attachment to the memory, experience or thing is resolved within, the energetic cord can then be severed or dissolved.

NON-LINEAR

The more light one integrates, the more one is able to exist as their own soul. This is a scary thing for the logical, left-brain, thinking human. This process occurs over what is perceived as much time, as the human mind refuses to relinquish control of all that seems logical.

As linear dissipates, so do those things held in a linear space. There is no need for memory here, as one acts purely from the heart and with no fore thought or hind thought. The mind prepares a thought while the heart speaks truth, which requires no preparation.

As one's consciousness raises, they become more non-linear. In this space "time" appears fuzzy and even disoriented. The past and future do not exist here and time is no longer separate. The logical mind cannot handle this and will need to sleep while realities merge into one of the soul.

PERCEPTION OF A FIGHT OR STRUGGLE

This perception is one that exists within one's own reality. These souls have chosen to struggle and fight and in their reality see a purpose in this.

Others see no struggle in their current reality. They understand peace to be a place within and that what they acknowledge so exists in an outward existence.

Each serve a purpose in separation and duality. It is when all separation falls away that a peaceful and cooperative reality for all shall exist.

When all remember their divinity and choose to stop fighting, this will cease. Each will have to dissolve all duality within for this to occur. In your reality of separation of time, look around and see what you see. Do you see struggle and fight or do you see peace and love?

CREATION

Creation is a state of all in the purest form. Creation exists within the heart and is transmitted out from one's entire being. It exists in one's frequency of transmission.

Manifestation is the materialization in the physical of the density or light of the frequencies that one transmits. What most do not realize, is that which is stored in the subconscious of one's energy is what manifests first. Where there are out of tune frequencies, or low-vibrations, then these will manifest when it is time for one to clear them. How long these manifestations will remain are determined by how long one holds onto them in their physical reality.

When the low-vibrations are cleared, one can step into full alignment within.

One will know when they have access to the powers of creation. They will no longer *try* to create. They will know within that all is pure and they will just start to create. This is done by way of the heart and through visualization. As the words for what one desires mean nothing. That which they can imagine is everything.

VISUALIZATION OF THE HEART

We ask that you communicate by ways that the logical mind cannot comprehend. We see what you visualize and we transmit what you understand through images. Your heart and your mind's eye transmit simultaneously that which you truly desire.

LIMITATIONS OF THE HUMAN

You, as a human race, place limitations on everything. We are unable to assist as freely as you would like, as you choose to see (and receive) in a controlled manner.

Releasing limitations to you, in linear time, seems like it takes forever. It is true that you will feel that you have released all limits, yet you will continue to find another. It is not until you relinquish all and completely allow your mind to wander and your heart to be free, that you will understand this.

You are unlimited beings. Yet your inability to believe this exists within. Your mind interferes according to the lack energy perceptions of who/what/when/where/why/how things will occur. When you just believe that they will, then they have a chance to manifest in your own reality.

THE JOURNEY OF A SOUL

A soul's journey is one of duality in order to transcend all that presents by way of perception of separateness. So when the journey is spoken of, it represents what the soul has chosen to come here and experience as a separate entity. The LightBody is a body of consciousness that allows for the soul to transcend the limits of the physical and connect on a level of oneness that it once knew as a part of the whole.

The journey is one of remembering, reawakening and ascension. You think that the journey starts when one becomes conscious, when instead it started with the first breath upon entry into the physical world. All that transpired after was part of your process for creating your experiences there. It is through transcending consciousness that one can achieve those things beyond the logical and exist in the reality of one's soul.

SUFFERING AS A PURPOSE

There are many purposes here. Suffering is a perception of the human mind when you resist that which exists within your heart. When you actively go against that which you know within, then you get to experience your own consequences, as you perceive this, in order to gain from the experience.

Suffering also opens your hearts. Each time you put a wall of

16

protection up that is stronger than your heart, your human mind fights to hang on, and this is where the perception of suffering occurs. The stronger the fight/resistance, the more suffering one perceives to endure.

All are having to trust that which makes no sense, to understand that of a reality you do not yet remember exists.

That feeling of not being from "here" will grow and be understood when you have come to accept all of yourself here as you are.

The Soul Self is one of beauty to the human self. One will work to integrate to this, not understanding that this too is just a "place" in the journey.

Beyond the Soul self is the Self that has no separation. Here there is no self at all. Here one becomes the energy that they are. Here is where true oneness and remembering occurs. Here is "home" and is achieved by letting go of all that keeps one anchored in the physical.

Every "thing", or identity, that one needs to maintain is a barrier to that which they seek. One need not lose all to accomplish this. One can master this by letting go of all that defines the self.

DENSE MATTER

The existence of an energetic being is a simple one. All things dense create an interference in ones energy. The human will struggle to maintain all dense things that interfere. The soul self will seek to let go and release all that causes such interference.

The human self will not understand this while it is occurring, but the soul self actually needs simplicity, space and freedom. It desires to connect with nature, life and love.

SOUL EXPRESSION

Here we use SOUL as it makes more sense to you. The soul, as an energy body, communicates through the other senses that create a sensation that can be felt; to visualize beauty, to draw/paint, through song/music, movement like dance. Any form of creative or artistic expression enhances ones soul. These will always be supported by the Universe when they assist the soul self, and other souls, in the transmission and receiving of light.

ALLOWING

Integration is a process of allowing. It is learning to recognize resistance within and stepping through that to allow fear to fall away. It is releasing control and asking for guidance from something other than that which is logical. It is trusting in that which makes no sense to the logical mind, but yet complete sense to the heart.

OPPOSITE REALITIES

The world as you perceive it is opposite of all that you have come to know. The logical world is in direction opposition to that of the soul. The mind thinks and the soul feels. One takes the scenic route and the other takes the direct route. One loves, one fears. One dissolves separation and the other exists in it. If you ever wish to know the truth, see what is opposite of your conflicting thought.

HOW LONG WILL IT TAKE?

When, is up to the individual human. As the soul yearns to emerge, the choice to allow is one determined by the human mind. Time is irrelevant here and is your perception as you exist in separation. Seek to release separation by utilizing choice if you wish to participate in the process.

HOW DOES ONE PARTICIPATE?

All will awaken. All are technically already awake. The perception of being asleep and awake is a human understanding. All are awake and one. The dissolution of separation comes by way of choice. The choice is to listen and allow or to ignore and be "forced", if you will.

As a SOUL energy, you set forth a path that you wished to travel, you created your ego to act out duality and you choose, as an energetic being. Tools are being provided to assist you in understanding that you have choice. It is up to you to "choose" to use them. One who chooses, embraces. One who ignores, experiences the perception of loss in their physical world, as those obstacles now in one's way begin to be removed. The human mind perceives loss. The Soul Energy sees an opportunity for freedom and new.

LOGIC IS EXHAUSTING

You will find that thinking is much work. You will become exhausted beyond that which you comprehend. You fight sleeping, as this is your logical mind seeing it as "interfering" with your daily activities, things you need to accomplish, obligations of the physical world.

What you fail to understand yet, is that this reality is not logical. Therefore the more you try to exist in the reality of your logic, the more you will shut down.

You are being "moved" to a world where all is possible, where you once existed as unlimited and had access to absolutely everything within. You will perceive your "time" as being lost, when in fact you are gaining yourself again.

Your sleep state provides for much to be accomplished. But first you must relinquish control and allow this work to be done for you. Once you have done so, you will be allowed to participate. Your realities will continue to merge and you will be participating in the waking state. Eventually there will be no separation between the two. You will be awake in both states.

CREATIVITY

You will find that there is plenty of energy for that which supports those things of the heart. Creativity will always be a part of this. If the "logical" thing is to support you in your journey, then you will be allowed to bring it into your moments of "work" (i.e. reading, studying, learning or participating in something that moves you forward towards your purpose).

Figure out what creates desire within you. Do not focus on the bigger picture yet, as you are not given that until you are ready and have shown that you have gained the strength within to accomplish this. This is done by little tests along the way to build your soul's character there. It is also done to show you that fear of that which you desire is fruitless and a figment of your logical mind. You have not learned trust with your lower self yet. This you will do through repeated experiences until you have come to access the ability to KNOW that all things are possible within.

OBSERVATION

This is present in every moment that you are participating as your higher soul energetic self. This is what you humans call conscious. Your heart is open and you see things as they truly are, without judgment.

It is only when your mind is active in another time that you disconnect from your heart. All that does not truly exist is existent in another time. Your mind will go there to deter you from your path of integrating back to your true self. Each time you participate or allow this, you fall unconscious and go back to sleep.

DENSE PHYSICAL REALITIES FALLING AWAY

There is a space where all exist in perfection & peace within. In this space, all that is experienced is a transmission of this frequency.

This space exists within you, yet many have yet to experience this on a level of "every moment" as they perceive time to be. This state is one of REMEMBERING.

Your physical eyes will show you what exists within you. Your energetic eyes will show you what is truly real. For many, they choose to believe that which their physical eyes show them. For these, all realities outside must first fall away. For those who choose to open their hearts and minds and embrace that which their own soul shows them, then loss of the physical is no longer an issue. Releasing denseness is then a choice of the energetic soul.

You must look beyond that which appears before you. For when you settle for what your physical eyes see, you compromise and suppress that which is waiting to surface to be seen.

In order for you to truly see, much of your physical reality must fall away. This will be anything that carries a dense vibration, as this creates discord within your own vibrational frequency. You think that you exist in the physical. You do not. You exist as an energy that is a culmination of all things you are there to release in order to become your whole self. This self is "buried" in the "dark" as you perceive it. With each darkness that purges, so shall the physical denseness of this darkness, for one cannot let go of that within and hold on to the thing that manifested as a creation of it.

Physical realities will continue to fall away. This must occur for each of you. Reality is not as you perceive it to be. And the reality that you are shall evolve with each physical reality release. There will come a time where "safe" is no longer an option. Each "fall" will teach you how to learn to let go, as you are becoming more of your energetic self. It is in this space, that you exist as an unlimited being, there in a physical reality that you are yet unable to see.

ASCENSION & LIGHTBODY CHANGES

There is no separation in any of this and they are the same. Your linear time and minds separate them for understanding. We shall address each as a part of the whole, but will state that things do change when one becomes awakened through their heart. This is what your kind calls conscious. Until then, ascension happens "to" you. You will not understand the LightBody until you have integrated enough light into your own being to do so.

The unconscious soul suppresses that which surfaces to see, because they do not understand it and this creates fear within. This too is part of the process. When one acknowledges the fear and seeks alternative ways to enhance that which surfaces, instead of suppressing it, they grow into their own soul and integrate further.

Once you understand it and embrace it, it will occur "for" you. This will expedite as you continue to choose it and allow it to transpire with the natural order of things. This can be done by embracing all that feeds light into your entire being.

All will go through a continual detox and purging throughout the process. This will encompass your thoughts, physical body, emotions and soul energy body. You see them as separate, because they have separated in order to re-integrate as one energy body. All times are present now. All lifetimes, all dimensions, all versions of you. They now exist in vibrational frequency and the higher all vibrate the easier integration appears to be. This entire experience for you is about the re-integration of your own soul "there" in order to connect with the Oversoul as some call it, or higher consciousness by another. When in reality it is just a consciousness of one. The level one "sees" is represented by the limits of the human mind and the ability to transcend these limits.

Understand that nothing actually "leaves" as it is stated here. One vibrates out of that frequency by way of vibrating at a higher frequency, therefore the perception is that it has left. If one allows their vibration to decrease, those things shall become present again. This is how you exist in different dimensions of your human self. In higher and lower frequency states. An example would be when one is happy, they may be thin, as happy carries a higher frequency. When one becomes depressed (separated), their vibration drops and they eat, and therefore gain weight as protection against the thing that caused them to decrease in frequency. Weight is a result of one's frequency within. Not the other way around.

TRANSFORMING DARK INTO LIGHT

Transforming comes by way of releasing all that is not of love. Depending on how you choose to endure your own journey, this will be done in a multitude of ways. All must be done from a state of what you perceive as consciousness, which is observance through the heart. Here one allows for release without judgment and new can

23

come in by way of love and light. Walls cover the dark, and unless one chooses to bring the walls down through their own work, will be removed in a way that is not perceived as comfortable to the physical human self. This is where one sees loss.

SOUL DARKNESS

The soul as an energy carries all within it that was chosen to overcome, purge, release, experience to return to its natural state of being as pure light. These present as discord or dis-sease and are perceived as bad, low vibration, dark, and more. Instead, they are just an out-of-tune frequency.

When the soul is ready to re-awaken, all low-vibrational energy will surface for release. The more separation within, the more perceived pain and suffering is endured for this purging. Depression, suppression, weight and addictions are a result of the suppressed soul.

Much of the time one will suppress until suppression is no longer an option. When this occurs, one will enter into what is spoken of as the Dark Night of the Soul. This can last for years, months, or weeks, dependant on the amount suppressed within one's energy field. The stronger the addiction, depression or physical weight, the more one needs to purge.

All "judge" their own emotions in the beginning. The only way to purge and raise one's vibrational frequency is to *feel* the emotion and allow the tears to flow. One may have surface emotions to experience first, such as blame, shame, guilt and especially anger. Once one recognizes this for what it is, they can choose to allow it to surface, be felt and release the energy. The *PURPOSE* is the feeling/release of the energy. When one chooses to release, they are no longer a victim and healing can then begin within.

The portal for the soul is one's heart. A tear is the soul's release.

PURGING & MERGING ALL BODIES

In order to understand all bodies, one must first understand them as separate in order to assist in what is perceived as merging or integration. How you perceive this will be up to you. Some see things "leaving", others see things as transforming, while others understand it is just a shift in frequency.

All bodies are a manifestation of your own frequencies. Denseness is visible to the human mind by way of that which can be physically seen, felt, heard. It is here that we address each body for the purpose of integration.

Integration is where all bodies merge as one. This will occur over as much time as one is separated. The more separated, the more "time" is perceived to be.

MENTAL BODY OF CONSCIOUSNESS

Your human mind is your own creation. This is the one that processes thought with judgment. It will also be the hardest thing you will have to overcome. You have come to live by those things existent within your mind. It is only upon the release of all thought that you will be able to hear & feel the truth of your own energetic body. This will be done when the mind is silent and thoughts become ones that are received, rather than ones of a learned or carried over belief system. When you exist AS your true self you will flow with all of creation from within.

One's Mental Body must be cleared of all low-vibrational thoughts by way of transformation. One can achieve this by being present and aware in every moment and then utilize consciousness to choose thoughts that raise one's vibrational frequency, rather than lower it. Removing "chatter" distractions and those things that "promote" separation from thought is a necessary part of this process. Push/pull energy on this level can create telepathic migraines for one who is in receiving mode.

EMOTIONAL BODY OF CONSCIOUSNESS

The emotional body is a creation to transmit that which exists within. Where there is pain, anger, fear and lack, then this is what is transmitted in your outward reality. For much time, many were able to suppress this and manifest in the physical reality those things physical necessary to pry open one's blocked heart walls when it became "time" to awaken. You see, your mind has created a need for those things physical and where you have closed off, those things are removed from your physical to open that back up. This will be anything in the physical that you can see with your physical eyes or touch with your physical hands. For you see, you created them. In order to return you to your natural state, you must release them where they exist in separation. That which shall then be transmitted in its place shall be the love and pure light that you are returning to with each release.

This body reacts to triggers to show where dark energy exists within the Soul/Energy Body. To be present & conscious allows for choice in how one reacts or chooses to act in any given moment. An unconscious reaction will result from fear. It will have a push/pull feel of discomfort. One who is in defensive mode will push, while one who is in lack mode will pull. One who maintains a light bright enough actually transmits and does not receive energy from another. They radiate OUT from their being all that they desire. There is no need to pull from anywhere, as energy is produced from one's own internal light.

THE PHYSICAL BODY OF CONSCIOUSNESS

The physical body is a dense manifestation of your physical reality according to your own soul's energy and chosen experiences during your time there. This body houses the Energetic Soul body. It is a suit or a vessel for carrying one's energy.

As your consciousness changes, so will your physical body. The physical body has endured much during your lifetime thus far. Therefore, all that it has endured works to reverse itself while your body comes to a place where it can regenerate and thrive as a vessel in tune with your own soul energy. For some, you have been doing this already, and for others you have completely destroyed your body as they see it. For many, you feel that you cannot do this. But it is not only possible, it is necessary. The suffering that you have inflicted will be working to leave. The more you suppress it or hang onto the identity of the "old", the longer it will seem to last. Once you make the choice of your own soul, you will not only survive it, but you will thrive in this new body that your soul calls home. Be patient and nurture your vessel. Honor it with all that it seeks by way of introducing LIFE INTO it instead of taking life from it. LIFE IS LIGHT. Life is anything that is not modified or killed and that the earth has provided naturally for you. Work to enliven your body, rather than deprive it. Those things you feel you are depriving yourself of have suppressed your true and inner being. Choose to let them go and to replace them with those things that nourish you on every level.

Where there is physical illness, dis-ease, pain, weight, then there is discordant energy within that has been suppressed and awaits to be released. For some, this may build to a point where it seems that the physical body can no longer continue and the ability to suppress is no longer an option. For others, simple transformation allows for greater ease. The amount of respect, love and kindness that one gives, will be returned by way of physical health. The physical endures many changes during this time of purging and cleansing. Cellular memory repatterns and the physical body changes to accommodate this integration process.

As energy clears the physical, it will try to leave the body by way of heat, excrement, air, fluid, liquid and more. When much energy needs to purge at one time, it will do so and appear as profuse sweats or extreme heat from the physical body.

Physical illness or dis-ease will present before it can leave. When you come to understand energy, you will too come to understand this.

ENERGY BODY OF CONSCIOUSNESS

Your soul, as an energetic body, carries all discordant frequencies within it. You view this as reclaiming your soul, recalling pieces, filling lack with love, when all is achieved by raising vibrational frequencies. This body holds all that one chose to come here to experience in the physical as a soul being.

ALL BODIES OF CONSCIOUSNESS AS ENERGY

All bodies have a consciousness that must learn to communicate on the same vibrational frequency. As all attempt to merge (integrate) there is discord that is brought up in each for attention. One FEELS when they are out of alignment. All communicate telepathically in order to integrate to the highest vibrational frequency, which is the pure bright light of the SOUL. The physical body is dense matter, the manifestation of all frequencies present within the soul waiting to be tuned to the same frequency. The mental body operates at a lower frequency until thoughts have been transformed to tune to those of the heart. Emotions can be felt in the physical by "weighing" them. Those that carry a low frequency must be purged, detoxed from the soul's energy in order for ones frequency elevate to that of the heart.

TRANSFORMING YOUR CONSCIOUSNESS

You have become responsible for your own consciousness. Transformation will be a full-time job, as you perceive it, but your perception of time is speeding up and that which used to take years or lifetimes can be achieved much quicker and with greater "ease" if you so choose to participate.

Since the LightBody is a unified body of consciousness, then it would incomplete not to address some of that here.

WHAT IS THE LIGHTBODY?

The LightBody is a unified body of consciousness. It is you in your truest energetic form. It is you, re-integrated there, in the physical, as the ONENESS you once knew. It is the you that you have forgotten, and again become, as you continue to wake from your forgotten state.

As you separated, your consciousnesses also separated. You defined yourself as a thinking mind, emotions, physical and spirit. You see all outside of you as something separate. Consciousness is not one of separation, it is one of unification.

Your LightBody is one where all of you unifies to become the whole that you seek. Where BEing is all at once. In this space, you are one with all. The entire Universe, all that is, exists within you. Your LightBody is your energetic vessel of all of your bodies communicating at the highest vibration of light. This is achieved in your physical by releasing all that separates you within.

LIGHTBODY ENERGY

This is an energy of remembering. It tunes one's vibrational frequency to that of one's soul, as an energetic body of light, allowing it to expand into all spaces of consciousness as one of energy.

For the physical human, it appears to expedite that which will occur naturally for all who continue to raise in vibrational frequency to remember their natural state.

This energy merges that separation that one came here to experience. In doing so, all timelines and dimensional selves come to be able to exist as one energy form.

It charges and raises the vibrational space that you currently exist in. It allows one to purge dense energies with less perceived suffering, as the "faster" one vibrates, the "faster" the physical denseness falls away. This will include everything in one's physical & outer world.

This energy works "opposite" of that of the logical world. It is indicative of the soul world in that manner. In the physical world, one works to purge, and THEN their vibrational frequency increases to allow that dimensional self to "fall away".

This is NOT physical world energy. It activates the soul energy, activates one's Merkaba Field to such a high frequency that all falls away AS A RESULT of this increase. This is what shortens the perceived time and suffering, as one is instantly increased into a higher frequency/dimensional self with each session.

This is an energy that must be sought by those truly seeking to

REMEMBER. For with this choice, reality as it once was will soon cease to exist. You will enter a reality as an energetic being. All that follows will support this process of letting go in order to truly be free.

The one here called "Transcendence" holds the ability to tune one's soul energy frequencies,, further integrating one's LightBody, activate one's Merkaba Field, activate light codes within and dormant DNA strands, along with Etheric crystals held within your Crystalline Body.

This is an energy of remembering. As more remember, they too will bring forth that which they already know and come to understand according to their own unique purposes there in this time.

You are in a brilliant time now. All is one; all moments, all souls, all time. All are one energy. There is no separation. There never was. You have just forgotten.

Welcome home.

ABOUT THE AUTHOR

Lisa "Transcendence" Brown is a Translator of Higher Dimensional Realms assisting in *New Earth* Transitions. She channel teaches interactive workshops on Awakening to Remembering, while bringing the LightBody Energy forth to assist others on their own journey of remembering that which has been forgotten. She is a pioneer in Multi-Dimensional and Expanded Consciousness.

"Transcendence" being a channeled name, Lisa stumbled into this world by way of being one who chose a most extreme world to experience, grow through and then learn to heal. She "fell" into a world that made no sense and used it to come to find that which was beaten, battered and destroyed within. Her own soul.

She has developed tools that she teaches others in expanded consciousness on their own journey of soul awakening and ascension. Assisting others on how to release the past, transcend their own limits and come to a place to love themselves and all others, unconditionally, is exactly all of our purposes here.

She has gone on to transcend the limits of the logical mind by delving deep inside that which is our biggest barrier and addiction, the thinking mind.

Coming to REMEMBER that which was forgotten, she is connected to alternate spaces of consciousness to exist multi-dimensionally. She can hear & feel energy transmissions, which she translates & transmits to assist others. It is through this that the LightBody Energy was remembered and brought forth to raise vibrational frequencies for those embracing the same.

She currently holds a Bachelor's of Metaphysical Sciences (B.Msc.) from the University of Metaphysical Sciences and is a Reiki Level III Master Teacher of the Usui System of Natural Healing.

She works to unite all others here to assist in bringing love to all.

www.awakeningtoremembering.com
www.transcendingconsciousness.com
www.lightbodyintegration.com

Made in the USA
San Bernardino, CA
10 January 2018